Balanced Scorecard
in a week

MIKE BOURNE
PIPPA BOURNE

Arnold

A HEADLINE GROUP

Acknowledgements

The authors and publishers would like to thanks the Engineering and Physical Sciences Research Council for their research grant which informed this work and the following organisations and people for the use of illustrations and information in this publication:

– Olive, N., Roy, J. & Wetter, M. (1999), *Performance drivers: a practical guide to using the balanced scorecard*. John Wiley & Sons: Chichester, UK.
– Lynch, R. L. & Cross, K. F. (1991), *Measure up – The Essential Guide to Measuring Business Performance*. Mandarin: London.
– Fitzgerald, L., Johnston, R., Brignall, T. J., Silvestro, R. & Voss, C. (1991), *Performance Measurement in Service Businesses*. The Chartered Institute of Management Accountants: London.
– The European Foundation for Quality Management.
– Bourne, M. C. S. & Wilcox, M. (1998), 'Translating strategy into action', *Manufacturing Engineer*, Vol. 77, No. 3, 109–112.

Orders: please contact Bookpoint Ltd, 130 Milton Park, Abingdon, Oxon OX14 4SB. Telephone: (44) 01235 827720. Fax: (44) 01235 400454. Lines are open from 9.00–17.00, Monday to Saturday, with a 24 hour message answering service. You can also order through our website www.hoddereducation.com

British Library Cataloguing in Publication Data
A catalogue record for this title is available from the British Library

ISBN-10: 0 340 849452
ISBN-13: 9780 340 849453

First published 2000
Impression number   10   9   8   7
Year   2007

Copyright © 2000, 2002 Mike Bourne and Pippa Bourne

Typeset by SX Composing DTP, Rayleigh, Essex.
Printed in Great Britain for Hodder Education, a division of Hodder Headline, an Hachette Livre UK Company, 338 Euston Road, London, NW1 3BH, by Cox & Wyman Ltd, Reading, Berkshire.

Hodder Headline's policy is to use papers that are natural, renewable and recyclable products and made from wood grown in sustainable forests. The logging and manufacturing processes are expected to conform to the environmental regulations of the country of origin.

■■■■C O N T E N T S■■■■

■ I N T R O D U C T I O N ■

The Balanced Scorecard proposed by Kaplan & Norton is over 10 years old now, but it is still not well understood by many. The objective of this book is to help you to develop and use the Balanced Scorecard to measure and improve your business performance. The maxim 'what gets measured gets done' really does work – but to make it work effectively you must measure the right things, otherwise you could find yourself spending a great deal of time on activities that are not contributing to your business success.

Over the last 10 years, companies have come to realise that they can no longer manage using financial measures alone. To survive and prosper, companies have to track non-financial measures, such as quality and speed of response; externally focused measures, such as customer satisfaction and brand preference; and forward looking measures, such as new product development and employee satisfaction. By having four distinct perspectives (financial, customer, internal process and innovation and learning) the Balanced Scorecard promotes a more holistic view of the business.

The Balanced Scorecard is a framework for designing a set of measures for activities chosen by you as being the key drivers of your business. For the scorecard to be effective you will need to display these measures and manage the resulting actions to improve performance. Over the next seven days we will take you through the various stages to help you to understand and implement an effective performance measurement system using the Balanced Scorecard.

Finally, in this updated edition, we will look to the future and present a new framework more appropriate for today's multi-stakeholder business environment.

The week ahead

Monday We look at getting started and the things you need to get right before you embark on a process to develop a performance measurement system.

Tuesday We will look at what to measure, how to decide what is important and how to clarify the business objectives.

Wednesday We will introduce you to a template to help you design your own measures, including a series of questions to ask yourself before you inflict them on your colleagues.

Thursday We will look at the use of performance measures, the tools and techniques to make them effective in your business and the visualisations to bring them alive.

Friday We will address some of the practical issues of performance measurement, giving examples of what can be achieved, as well as potential pitfalls and setbacks.

Saturday On the final day we will complete the picture by giving examples of how companies have adapted the Balanced Scorecard to their own business needs. But we will also explain how performance measurement is progressing beyond the scorecard and introduce the Performance Prism, a new stakeholder oriented framework.

What is the Balanced Scorecard?

Today we look at:
- the reasons for measuring performance
- what the Balanced Scorecard is
- what type of organisations can use the Balanced Scorecard
- an overview of the remainder of the week

Why measure performance?

The ultimate aim of implementing a performance measurement system is to improve the performance of the organisation – and there is evidence to show that this is the case. One study by Lingle and Schiemann found that 'measure-managed companies' performed better than others in three important aspects. They were perceived as

being industrial leaders, providing higher financial returns and being adept at managing change.

A good measurement system will help you to achieve success in five ways. It will help you to:

- establish your current position
- communicate direction
- stimulate action in the most important areas for your business
- facilitate learning
- influence behaviour

Establishing your current position
This is important because you need to know where your starting point is. What is the basic health of the organisation? What is the level of performance against which you will judge improvement? What are your strongest/weakest points?

Unless you measure accurately and consistently, the whole ethos of measurement will be undermined. Before you start making comparisons between departments or between your company and someone else's you need to establish your current position through clearly defined and appropriate performance measures. Establishing your current position, then, is a vital first step in performance measurement.

Communicating direction
This concerns deciding and communicating where you are going and what is important to the organisation. We have said 'what gets measured gets done'. By creating a set of measures you are already indicating what is important and

where people should concentrate their efforts because this is how their own performance will be judged. A good measurement system can provide a clear set of measurable goals and timescales for achieving them based on the organisation's strategic plan. By gaining commitment to the measures and publicising them, it is possible to create a culture of achievement, one in which individuals are no longer working in the dark but know what is expected of them and can see the progress they are making.

How many times have you seen a well-constructed strategic plan, created and read by a few but ineffectively communicated across the business? Performance measurement can rectify this, making the goals and objectives explicit, bringing the strategy to life and communicating directions throughout the whole business.

Stimulating action in key areas
This ensures that time and energy is spent on issues that are most important for the business. The measurements should show where effort should be directed. It is important to note here that measures are not static, they evolve. As one result becomes stronger, attention may be given to another weaker area. Regular measurement also highlights at an early stage any trends affecting the business, making it possible to take action before it is too late.

Just remember that if no action is taken as a result of measurement, the whole impetus is lost.

Facilitating learning
This is an important part of the performance measurement process. Having a set of measures is one thing, but the real benefit comes from reflecting on what the measures are

telling you and deciding what action you should take. Using a good set of measures to provoke debate about key issues of the business strategy can help decision-making and thus drive the business forward.

There are two important questions you should ask yourself:

> - Do the measures show how well you are implementing your strategy?
> - Do the measures show that the strategy is broadly correct?

The measures should give you information to help you answer both these questions but it will only happen if you take the time to review and reflect, using the measures to facilitate your learning.

Influencing behaviour
This is about encouraging the right behaviour and discouraging inappropriate actions. If correctly devised and communicated, measures can motivate individuals to achieve the organisation's goals and targets. Implementing measures affects behaviour just by focusing attention on key areas.

Measures that are badly constructed, however, can destroy an organisation's performance. This can happen when improving the performance of the activity being measured does not improve the performance of the business as a whole. In this case, effort may be misdirected into unproductive actions and a great deal of time and effort can be wasted.

To conclude, implementing a performance measurement system can have far-reaching effects on the organisation. It can be used for:

- deciding what the key drivers of performance are
- refocusing and stimulating activity on these key business drivers
- drawing attention to goals and targets
- creating a culture of achievement
- noticing in advance any trends affecting the business so that changes can be made in good time.

Before implementing the system, then, it is clearly very important to agree and design a good set of measures and to gain commitment to them. The measures influence behaviour and activity so your level of success will largely depend on how well you have set up your system.

What is the Balanced Scorecard?

In the 1980s many academics and consultants became concerned that too much emphasis was being put on financial and accounting measures of performance. Management accounting systems had been perfected to produce detailed cost breakdowns and extensive variance reports but these were seen as not being useful for managing a business because they were too internally focussed and were backward looking.

To overcome these shortcomings various academics and consultants started to consider the concept of balance. Among these were Robert Kaplan and David Norton who popularised the idea of a Balanced Scorecard, initially in the United States.

Kaplan and Norton identified four perspectives each

representing an important face of the organisation. These were:

- financial
- external customer
- internal process
- innovation and learning

Their idea was that these four perspectives represent a balanced view of any organisation and that by creating measures under each of these headings no important area would be missed. It is important to remember that the scorecard itself is just a framework and it doesn't say what the specific measures should be. That is a matter for people within the organisation to decide, and the set of measures for each organisation (or even sections within the same organisation) will be different. Much of the success of the scorecard depends on how the measures are agreed, the way they are implemented and how they are acted upon. So the process of designing the scorecard is just as important as the scorecard itself.

A typical scorecard for a manufacturing company looks something like Figure 1.

In business it is accepted that the financial needs of the business have to be met. At the most basic level there must be cash flow to sustain the enterprise. Beyond this, the business must provide the cash to cover any interest on its debts. Finally, the shareholders or owners are looking for a return on their investment.

However, focusing purely on financial aspects is not

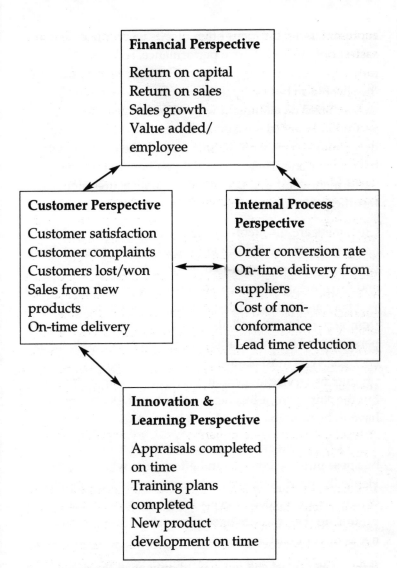

Figure 1, A typical Balanced Scorecard for a manufacturing company

enough. Firstly, the focus often results in people taking the easiest options to improve performance, reducing costs rather than encouraging growth. This may be beneficial in the short term but in the longer term, cuts in investment, research and development will harm the business. Secondly, financial measures are 'result measures', that is, they provide a measure of how well all the other activities have been done. They do not tell you how to improve performance and that is why financial measures alone are insufficient to manage the business.

Customers are the lifeblood of the business, their orders and payments are the reason for the business to exist. It is therefore very important to understand the needs of current and prospective customers so you know why they buy from you now and what will determine whether they will buy from you in the future. This is why you need the *customer* perspective. However, satisfying customers in itself is not enough. At its most absurd level you could give your product or service away to the delight of your customers but the ruin of your business! Other business objectives have to be brought in to create a balance.

To satisfy customers and make a financial return, the business must be efficient and effective at what it does. Hence the third perspective, *internal process*. The objective here is not to be good at everything but to be brilliant at producing the products or services which match the exact needs of your customers.

If the world stood still, we would only need three perspectives, but, as we know, it changes constantly. To keep up with the ever increasing demands of your customers and the ever improving performance of your competitors you need to *innovate and learn*. The fourth perspective is all about developing the capabilities and processes you will need for the future. This perspective often contains most of the measures for people development.

The four perspectives are designed to balance:

- the financial and the non financial
- the internal and the external
- current performance with the future

More recently, the Balanced Scorecard has been developed to make the links between the individual measures more explicit. This has been done by developing what is called a

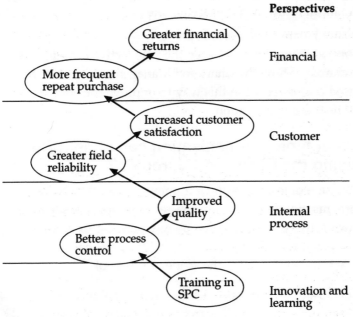

Perspectives

Financial

Customer

Internal process

Innovation and learning

Figure 2, An example of a partial business model

'Business Model' which links improvements in one area with those in another.

Let us take a simple example. A company may believe that training in SPC (statistical process control) may improve control over its manufacturing processes. It is believed that this increase in control will increase the quality of a product. This improvement in quality may be thought to improve product reliability in the field and this might be reflected in increased customer satisfaction. As a result, customers may make more repeat purchases which will increase sales volumes and drive up financial returns (see Figure 2). Such a business model cuts across all the perspectives of the Balanced Scorecard. In the example above, it links an innovative training programme with the financial return to the shareholder.

Many Balanced Scorecards are now represented in pictorial form showing links between the perspectives. Figure 3 is an example of how the Chartered Management Institute has used the scorecard in this way to improve the effectiveness of its training operation.

What type of organisation can benefit from using the Balanced Scorecard?

As the scorecard is really a framework into which the organisation fits a set of measures most appropriate to its own activity, it can be used by any business or service provider. It could even be adapted for personal, individual use but that is outside the scope of this book.

The beauty of this approach lies in its flexibility. The framework provides the necessary structure but the detail can be tailored precisely to the needs of any organisation.

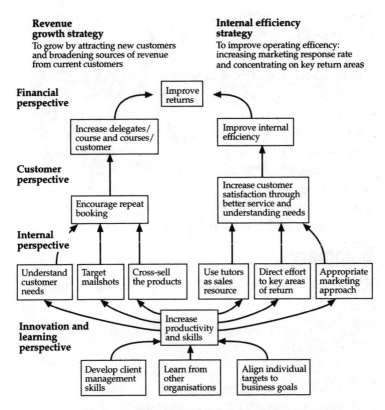

Figure 3, A version of the Balanced Scorecard developed for the Chartered Management Institute Training Operation

The Balanced Scorecard was originally developed for the business sector, for profit-oriented organisations. However, there is no reason why it shouldn't be used for charities or public sector organisations. A simple way of adapting the Balanced Scorecard for such organisations is by swapping the positions of the customer and financial perspectives. In this way the objective is to maximise the service provided to customers within the constraints of the available finances.

ALL OF THEM
FIT THE DESCRIPTION

Summary

A good performance measurement system should include:

- a balance of financial and non financial performance measures
- a balance of internal and external measures
- a balance of past achievement measures and measures which help to predict the future
- a consistent set of measures which create a firm base for measuring progress or making comparisons
- a unique set of measures which communicates the strategic direction, goals and targets
- a mechanism which stimulates action from the results of the measures
- a mechanism for reviewing and learning from the information the measures provide

How to begin

Today we look at how to get started, in particular at:
- creating the right environment for success
- gaining commitment
- who should be involved

Creating the right environment for success

As with all projects and processes, it is important to get off
to a good start and to encourage those involved by showing
them some early benefits. This means devoting a substantial
amount of thinking time at the beginning to the factors that
will create a successful start. This really is time well spent
because it will take even more time to gain people's
commitment after a rocky beginning.

Stage 1: Define your scope
So, where do you begin? Think first about the scope and

purpose of the process. Why are you doing it and what area of your business will it cover? Logically, it makes sense to put top level measures in place first. These are measures linked to the strategy of the business as a whole, the strategy of a subsidiary business or product line or a department. What is important is that there is a clearly defined area of the business where you can set overarching goals in line with the strategy. It is possible to do a bottom-up approach to performance measurement but these naturally focus on local departmentally-based improvements which have less impact (although, they do have an impact and can be done later).

If you are the instigator of the process you need to be in a situation where you can set your own objectives otherwise you will have to negotiate agreement to do this so that the process is not undermined by an initiative at a more senior level.

Stage 2. Think of the groups of people from whom you need support and what the benefits are for them.
When you have defined your scope you will have a clearer understanding of the groups of people from whom you will need commitment. It is worth spending a little time considering who these people are and what they will want from the process. Whether you decide to opt for a top-down or a bottom-up approach you still need support from the senior management team. Designing and implementing a performance system using the Balanced Scorecard takes considerable investment in time and cannot be done effectively in isolation. The senior team should help to facilitate this.

In order to make effective use of the results you get from using the process you need commitment from your staff and there may be other groups of people you will need to influence in your particular circumstances. The second part of this section deals with tactics for gaining this commitment – at this stage just think of the people from whom you need support.

Stage 3. Get your timing right

Another important factor is getting your timing right. What other initiatives are there in the business at present? If you are going through a major restructuring programme, now may not be the time to embark on something else – gaining commitment from colleagues and staff alike may well be difficult!

Also consider the start time for implementing the Balanced Scorecard. If you start at the year end or budget review time you are less likely to get support because others are too busy.

Finally, if your organisation is facing a crisis of some type then now is probably not the time to implement the

Balanced Scorecard. It is an investment for the future and benefits tend to be longer term. In a crisis there are other, more appropriate ways of generating the necessary short-term gains.

Stage 4. Consider the relationship with the organisation's strategy and with other strategic initiatives.

The next point to consider is where the process fits into the strategic planning cycle. The Balanced Scorecard should give some clarity and measurement to the strategic plan and help in its implementation. Also think about the relationship with any other initiatives going on in the organisation. Over the last few years, many people have claimed to be suffering from initiative overload – Total Quality Management, Business Process Reorganisation, Investors in People.... What next? Don't let the Balanced Scorecard be seen simply as another in a series of one-off projects with a start, middle and end. It should be seen as a follow-on to these initiatives rather than as something entirely new, as a tool which will help in implementing TQM or Investors in People or the business strategy. By building on previous projects, the Balanced Scorecard can become woven into the daily management of the business.

Gaining commitment

We believe the most effective use of the Balanced Scorecard is to help people to measure their own effectiveness in key areas of the business and to use these measures to improve performance. In some organisations measures are used as a way of grading the performance of individuals or to create competition between comparable sections of the business – such as setting up league tables between different branches.

The problem here is that it is likely to meet with resistance and it will probably turn into a competition to get the best measure results rather than a genuine team effort to improve the business.

This book focuses on a more participative approach to using the Balanced Scorecard by winning over the management and staff teams to using measures as a good way of managing performance of the business. In order to do this you must stress the benefits to the individual.

It is important to remove, as far as is reasonable, the threat of personal blame for individuals. In high blame cultures people fear performance measurement systems because they risk unpleasant criticism. In this climate they are unlikely to be entirely open about the results and may hinder the measurement process. One way to overcome this is to concentrate objectively on the business issues and associated process problems rather than focusing on individual weaknesses.

In the initial discussions there may be difficult issues that have to be aired before the process can move forward to the final outcome of the creation of a set of effective performance measures and objectives. Major political problems which arise later can cause trouble so it is useful to raise them at the initial stage and find a way of resolving them.

Who should be involved

If you are adopting a top-down approach then the whole of the senior management team needs to be involved because you are measuring the business as a whole. If you leave someone out, you not only lose their input, you also lose the commitment and support from that part of the business. You can't delegate the exercise of agreeing and designing the measures to a staff team. If senior line managers are not involved, the initiative will be perceived as being unimportant.

When you cascade the measures down through the business others can be involved at appropriate stages in the process.

The next question to consider is whether to use an external consultant to guide you through the process. There are, of course, advantages and disadvantages to using an external consultant or facilitator and you will have to decide according to the circumstances prevailing in your organisation.

Using an external consultant or facilitator

Advantages
- provides an objective point of view
- brings experience of using the process with other

organisations which may increase your chances of success
- provides facilitation skills to manage debate and challenge existing mindset
- provides additional time and resources

Disadvantages
- could be expensive
- may not understand your business
- the 'chemistry' may not fit with your management team
- can be difficult for an outsider to be accepted – 'not invented here'

Whether you decide to use an external consultant or not, you will need an internal project manager responsible for the day-to-day management of the project and to act as the interface with the external consultant if you decide to appoint one. This person will ensure that the administration runs smoothly and should also act as another 'internal champion' for the project. The project manager should report to the project sponsor – the senior manager or director who can use authority to get things done when necessary.

Summary

In this chapter we have looked at ways in which to create the right environment to start using the Balanced Scorecard effectively. You need to:

- define the scope of business to be measured using the Balanced Scorecard
- think about the people from whom you will need support to implement the project successfully and consider their needs – this will help you to gain their commitment
- get your timing right – don't start a major new project if you are involved in too many other initiatives
- consider the relationship with the organisation's strategy and with other strategic initiatives – the Balanced Scorecard can be used to help implement strategic initiatives
- try to give political problems an airing at an early stage, this will help you to avoid problems later
- stress the benefits of the scorecard as a tool for managing the performance of the business and not as a stick with which to threaten individuals
- involve the whole senior management team
- appoint a project manager to manage the day-to-day running of the project during the start-up phase

Deciding what is important

In the last chapter we looked at how to create the right
environment for success and gave an overview of how to
begin the process of using the Balanced Scorecard. Now it is
time to think about the measures themselves and what to
measure.

Today we will show:

- ways of identifying the needs of the various
  stakeholders in the business
- how to decide on key drivers of business
  performance
- how to measure the right things

Perhaps *the* most important factor for success in using the
Balanced Scorecard is ensuring that you are measuring the
right things. If you measure the wrong things you can
channel energy and time into activities that are not

contributing towards the success of your business, with damaging results. The second task of your project team (after agreeing the scope of what is to be covered by the project and who to involve) is to decide what should be measured.

Analysing needs

How do you decide what is important for your business? The following is a simple framework designed to help you clarify your thinking.

One basic requirement for success is identifying and satisfying your customers' needs in line with your business strategy. Your customers will have a set of requirements and your business strategy will have been created to take account of these. But you will also need to take account of other requirements including the needs of stakeholders such as shareholders, employees or even the local community, depending on the nature of your business. There are two approaches you can take from here:

IGNORE YOUR STAKEHOLDERS AT YOUR PERIL

1. Look at the strategy and extrapolate from this what the key factors are to ensure you achieve strategic aims.
2. Analyse the needs of the stakeholders to ensure you are really focusing on the most important factors for success.

If you are confident that your strategy reflects your stakeholders' needs then this may be your starting point. If not, then it is as well to go back to consider the needs of the various interested parties in your business. These may include:

- customers
- consumers
- employees
- shareholders
- owners
- regulators
- the local community
- suppliers

We will take the analysis of customer need as an example of how to think this through.

The idea here is not to consider every detail – the exercise would take much too long – but to think about the most important requirements that particular group will have from your business. The next question to ask is *how do you know these are the requirements?* We often assume we know what other groups want and sometimes it is worth checking that our understanding is correct.

Example – What do your customers want?

Parkway Motor Sales and Service is a large dealership which has, in the past, been making most of its profits from servicing customers' cars. Profits from this section of the business have fallen quite considerably recently, much to the surprise of the general manager who has made it her particular concern to set high standards for procedures and customer service. She has been running regular training courses for all employees concerned with servicing cars. These courses have included a session on customer needs and how to meet them, with a list of actions to be taken when servicing a car. These were stated as:

- all work to be completed to service specifications by the required time
- protection to be placed over car seats and steering wheel to avoid oil stains
- car to be cleaned before return to customer
- cars to be parked near the front of the forecourt when service has been completed so the customer can drive away easily
- friendly and personal service

Despite these actions fewer people were returning their cars to Parkway for servicing. In desperation, the general manager decided to do a customer survey to find out what had gone wrong. Results showed customers wanted the following:

- full-day working on Saturday (or use of courtesy car) because they need their own cars during the week to travel to work – Saturday appointments at Parkway are booked weeks ahead and the two courtesy cars are always in use
- fast processing of paperwork so they can collect

their cars quickly and drive away – queues at Parkway can be quite long, meaning a delay before they can return home at the end of the day
- lower costs generally and a telephone call to seek the customer's permission to go ahead with work above a certain cost level – some customers had a nasty shock when they came to pay their bills!

Armed with this knowledge, the general manager was able to make changes to ensure customers were satisfied and returned to Parkway for their servicing.

Checking your understanding of needs may involve commissioning market research or it may simply involve talking to a sample of customers. Either way it will help to ensure you are focusing on the most productive factors. The following exercise will help you to improve your understanding of customer needs and prioritise your actions for improvement.

(a) Make a list of what you think is important to your customers (or most important group of stakeholders)

(b) Grade on a scale of 1–10 how you think you perform on each of these points

(c) Think of your key competitors and grade how you think they perform on the same points

(d) Ask a representative sample of your customers what is important to them and ask them to grade your performance

This is a useful exercise because it shows any mismatch between customers' requirements and the focus of attention of the business. Look at the following example from a company manufacturing windows:

Attribute	company performance	competitor performance	customer importance rating
delivery on time and in full	5	7	9
length of delivery lead time	9	6	6
choice of styles	9	8	7
quality of window fitments	9	8	9
low price	6	8	8
customer aftercare	6	7	9

Clearly there are several mismatches in this example. The company has focused on achieving a short delivery lead time when what is really important to the customer is having delivery in full on the agreed date. Would it have been better, perhaps, to have had a slightly longer lead time and to have used the extra time to ensure that there were no mistakes on delivery?

Who is the customer?

Just a note of caution here – it is important to understand the differing needs of customers and consumers. Take the following example of the purchase of a toy where the purchaser (customer) is the parent and the consumer is the child. There is no doubt that there will be distinct differences in the needs and wants of these two groups. The child may well have no concerns whatsoever about noise levels (the noisier the better perhaps....). Features potentially damaging to the fabric of the house such as stickiness or sharp edges may, in the child's eyes, be benefits! The parent, on the other hand will look at features such as durability, safety and value for money. This certainly leads to issues for consideration by the marketing department but it is also important to develop an understanding of the different customers and

	House owner	Architect	Builder	Builder's merchant
Quality	Must last Must look nice	Special effects for interesting designs Must look nice	Easy to lay Undamaged on arrival	Doesn't want returns
Cost	Quite important for overall price of house	Less important	Erected cost important	Interested in profit margin
Time	Important that house is completed on time	No particular concern	Must arrive when promised Short lead time	Must arrive when promised Short lead time
Flexibility	No particular interest	Wide product range from which to choose	No particular concern	Wide product range to attract wide range of customers

Figure 4, The differing needs of consumers and customers

consumers for the purposes of implementing the Balanced Scorecard.

Figure 4 above is an example of the different needs of customers and consumers of a brick manufacturer.

Having analysed the needs of the various stakeholders, the next step is to use this information to decide what really affects the success of your business, using the four perspectives of the Balanced Scorecard as a framework for thinking about the objectives and measures under each section. Clearly these will be peculiar to your business but here is a simple example of a Balanced Scorecard.

The Eden Landscape Gardening Company

The Eden Landscape Gardening Company has recently changed hands. It is a well-established business situated in a leafy area of Worcestershire where there is a significant number of large houses and select executive developments. The previous owner was a very keen gardener rather than a businessman and built up the business to the point where he employed 30 gardeners, using his contacts and reputation to attract new business from all over the country. Although the business has shown some growth over the last two years, profits have been falling. Two rival firms have been set up during this time by former employees who do not have his overheads, whereas before there had been virtually no competition.

The new owner has been working on a strategic plan

and has decided that his key aims will be to achieve profitable growth of existing services but with a move 'up-market' to a higher price/quality segment of the market and an increased market share within a 25-mile radius of his office.

He is keen to measure how well he is progressing towards achieving his strategic aims and has decided to use The Balanced Scorecard as a framework for doing this.

Financial Perspective

Objective: to achieve profitable growth
Measures: growth in net sales; return on assets; average order value; value of sales per employee

Customer Perspective:

Objective: to gain a reputation specifically for high-quality and reliable service; to be the gardener of choice for landscape projects between £10,000–£50,000.
Measures: the conversion rate from enquiries to contracts within the specified value range; the number of referrals for business, percentage of annual maintenance contracts renewed

Internal Perspective:

Objective: to reduce journey time to and from each customer; to increase efficiency
Measures: journey time as a percentage of time worked; value of capital equipment as a percentage of turnover; salaries as a percentage of turnover

---

Innovation and Learning Perspective:
Objective: *to increase the quality of work done; to keep abreast of new developments in gardening*
Measures: *number of days training per employee; employee satisfaction; number of suggestions from employees for new designs*

Identifying the key drivers of the business – the 'what/how' approach

The what/how approach is a simple technique for translating a top-level business goal into the series of sub-objectives necessary to achieve this goal. It is the approach adopted by Kaplan & Norton in their book 'The Balanced Scorecard, Translating Strategy into Action', and variations of this approach have been used by companies such as BT.

The idea is to encourage debate between the members of the senior management team around the core objective of the organisation. Once this has been agreed, you should steer the debate from 'what is to be achieved' to 'how should this be achieved'.

Let's take an example. Your company wishes to increase its financial returns – the "what". Your management team may see two main methods of achieving this – the "hows". These are increasing revenues and reducing costs. See Figure 5.

Your management team will now turn to the question of how to increase the revenues and how to cut costs. The 'hows' for increasing returns now become the 'whats' for the next level down.

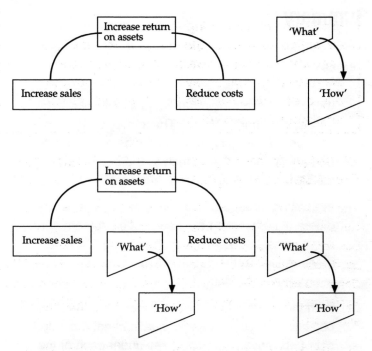

Figure 5, A 'what/how' example

In this way the 'hows' and 'whats' of achieving the strategy are cascaded down the business. By doing this you are creating a business model, encapsulating how your managers believe action at one level affects outcomes at the next level, drawing the belief into a cause and effect diagram which communicates the strategy.

This is a useful technique for developing an explicit version of your business strategy creating the top-level objectives.

Summary

In this chapter we have looked at how to decide what to measure.

- Identify the most important factors that will create success in your business. These may be apparent from your strategic plan or it may be necessary to go back to identify and analyse the needs of the various stakeholders in your business.

- In thinking about the needs of these stakeholders, differentiate between the needs of customers and consumers – and ensure as far as you can that these really are the needs not just your interpretation of them.

- With the needs of your stakeholders and the key objectives of your strategic plan in mind, draw up a set of objectives and measures under each of the four perspectives of the Balanced Scorecard. Be careful to consider fully the implications of the measures you have chosen.

How to measure

Today we look at the design of the measures themselves including:

- problems with measures
- the performance measurement record sheet
- examples of measures
- designing groups of measures

Problems with measures

Many people think the process is over once you have set the objectives, but this is not the case. You need to design your measures carefully as is demonstrated by the real life example below.

An airline was concerned that an important aspect of customer satisfaction was determined not by the flight itself, but by how quickly the passengers received their luggage after landing. As a result, the company set an objective to improve baggage delivery speed and introduced a performance measure in an attempt to support this new initiative.

After this performance measure was introduced, a team of baggage handlers was observed in action at the airport and this is what happened.

The team of baggage handlers stood around chatting and smoking in a group awaiting the tractor pulling the baggage cars from the aeroplane. As the tractor arrived, the team leader sprang into action. He grabbed a small bag off the first car and threw it to the youngest member of the team, who caught the bag and them sprinted across the tarmac. On reaching the baggage conveyor, he threw the bag on to it and then relaxed, sauntering back to the rest of the group. The other baggage handlers were unmoved by this frenetic activity and were still engrossed in their conversation which they continued until they had finished their cigarettes. It was only when the chatting and smoking were finished that the whole team started to unload the cars.

The company started correctly by trying to improve customer service and identifying the main determinants of customer satisfaction, one of which was 'quick delivery of customers' baggage'. However, the measure was inappropriate. By putting the emphasis on the time for the first bag to arrive, they failed to get the behaviour they desired.

Clear thinking is vital for deciding what to measure. When taken at face value, there are some measurements which seem eminently suitable but, if taken in isolation or taken to their logical conclusion, may in fact be damaging.

A measure of the overall number of delegates attending courses each month is proposed for a provider of training courses. As two of the company's objectives are firstly to be seen as a leading provider of management development and secondly to make a profit, this measure seems appropriate.

The underlying assumptions are: (a) the more delegates who attend the better because more people are aware of the company's services, and (b) the increased number of delegates increases the profit.

The act of measuring and therefore putting emphasis on attracting a larger number of delegates will influence the strategy for marketing, pricing and determining the events offered. The outcome might possibly be a series of cheaper, lower quality courses attended by more people attracted by a highly expensive marketing campaign. This could lead to a worsening of the financial position and people so disillusioned with management development that they will never attend another course – the opposite of the desired outcome.

In this case it is questionable whether the number of delegates is a useful measure. If it is to be used then, given the organisation's objectives, it should be balanced against measures of profitability and quality.

When designing measures, you need to consider:

- what behaviour will this encourage?
- is this behaviour desirable?

Today we focus on the important task of designing performance measures. The framework we will use is the performance measurement record sheet developed by Andy Neely and his colleagues at Cambridge University. This asks a series of questions which you should answer in designing each measure. We will then use examples to demonstrate the use of the record sheet.

The performance measurement record sheet

A blank example of the record sheet is shown in figure 6 and a description of each box is given on the next page.

There are many good reasons for completing a performance measurement record sheet:

Establishing position

- it fully documents the measure, so everyone knows precisely how it is to be calculated
- it establishes the frequency of measurement
- it identifies the individual responsible for measuring and the source of data so that the measure can be

measured consistently, an important point if results
are to be compared between two periods

Communicating direction

- it explains why we are measuring this
- it connects performance measures to top-level
  organisational objectives, making the link clear
- it defines precisely what is to be achieved and by
  when

Influencing behaviour

- designing the measure signals that management is
  interested in this aspect of the organisation's
  performance

Stimulating action

- it identifies who is responsible for taking action to
  ensure performance improves
- it identifies in outline the first steps in making an
  improvement

Facilitating learning

- just completing the record sheet will help
  understanding and often leads to new insights

Measure title	
Purpose	
Relates to	
Target	
Formula	
Frequency	
Who measures?	
Source of data	
Who acts on the data?	
What they do?	
Notes and comments	

Figure 6, The performance measurement record sheet (adapted from Neely et al, 1996)

The Performance Measurement Record Sheet

Title
You should give every measure a title which captures its essence

Purpose
Why are you measuring this? If you can't produce a good reason, then maybe you shouldn't measure this at all. This should guide you when you review the

measures answering the two questions, 'what
behaviour will this encourage?' and 'is this desirable?'

Relates to

To what top-level business objective does this
measure relate? You should design measures to
support the achievement of the top-level objectives –
often managers are inclined to insert measures which
will show them (or their department's performance) in
a good light! By linking the measure to the top-level
business objectives, this question prevents you
making the same mistake.

Target

What performance target should be set? Your targets
should also include a time frame for reaching them.
Everything you have learnt before about targets being
'high but achievable' needs to be applied here.

Formula

How is the performance measure calculated? Be
precise – too often people are inclined not to include a
formula and as a result the IT department makes the
decision. Your formula must include precisely what
you are measuring or you may get a result like the
baggage handlers' example above.

Frequency

You should decide how often this is to be measured
and how often the measure is to be reviewed.

Who measures

You must identify who is responsible for measuring
this performance.

Source of data
You should specify the source of the data so that the measure is taken consistently. In this way you can compare performance between periods.

Who takes action
You must allocate responsibility for taking action on this measure.

What do they do
You should be able to specify in outline the types of action your people should take to improve the performance of this measure. If you can't describe this then you are asking too much of your people.

Notes and comments
You will find it useful to record any additional notes and comments here. For example, if the target was a pure guess, you may want to note that you should be reviewing it again once the measure has been in use for 3 months.

Useful tip
On Tuesday we suggested that the senior management team of the organisation should work together to develop a mutually agreed set of objectives. These can be expressed simply, for example, 'increase the percentage of our orders delivered on time to over 95%' or 'reduce customer waiting time to under 5 minutes at all times'. The management team involved in setting these objectives may have a clear idea of what the organisation needs to achieve but lacks the detailed knowledge to design an appropriate performance measure.

If the measure owner involves a group of managers and other knowledgeable employees in the design of the measure, this will help with the practicalities of measurement, communicate what is important and explain why it is important. It will also start to involve others in the performance measurement project and facilitate the roll out of the measures to the rest of the organisation.

Examples of measures

Four examples of measures are described here, one for each perspective of the Balanced Scorecard. We have given the examples to highlight some of the pitfalls you will meet in designing performance measures. But don't be put off by these, it isn't easy to design a perfect performance measure and you are not striving for perfection. Just be aware of the shortcomings of your measures and be prepared to change them later.

Financial – return on capital employed (see Figure 7)
Almost any accounting text book will tell you how to calculate your return on capital employed (ROCE), but in this case, the accounting accuracy is less important than understanding the impact the measure will have when used within your organisation. (Obviously, if you are making external comparisons, the measure may well have to be calculated differently, but beware when comparing 'raw' measures between organisations. Measures have often been adapted to suit a particular purpose and unless fully understood they are not comparable at all.)

Your desired outcome from this measure is probably that your organisation increases its return on capital employed, either by earning greater profits or by more efficient use of the capital employed. This will spur your management team to increase sales, reduce costs and manage their working capital.

However, the same result could be achieved through:

- delaying capital investment which is in the interest of longer term efficiencies and cost savings
- delaying research and development projects which don't give a return this year
- reducing advertising expenditure which will only have a small impact in the short term
- reallocating overheads

These all increase the short term ROCE but may well damage your business in the longer term. The idea of having a Balanced Scorecard is to counteract many of these problems. This is done by including in the scorecard other measures for increased operating efficiency, new products developed on time, brand awareness and so on. But there are still questions which need to be asked about this measure.

- Are the earnings used here earnings before tax, interest, depreciation, central overheads ...?
- Which earnings can the management team influence?
- Which costs are simply a distraction (e.g. allocated central overheads)?

So you need to decide what is the most appropriate earnings figure to be included in the measure. The ideal measure will reflect fairly the outcome of the combined effort of the whole management team.

Performance Measurement Record Sheet

Measure	Return on capital employed
Purpose	To focus on the returns being made on the capital employed and careful use of working capital
Relates to	The need for the business to make an adequate return to its investors
Target	Achieve a rate of return of over 20% by the end of 2000
Formula	$$\frac{\text{Profit before tax and interest}}{\text{Net capital employed}} \times 100$$
Frequency	To be measured monthly, to be reviewed quarterly
Who measures?	Bill Jones, Finance Director
Source of data	Monthly management accounts
Who acts on the data?	Roger Morris, Ops Director; Raymond Smith, Sales Director
What do they do?	Manage finished goods and WIP, manage production costs, review sales margins
Notes and comments	

Figure 7, Return on capital employed

External – customer complaints (see figure 8)
The recording and analysis of customer complaints is an
activity undertaken by most businesses and a requirement
of the ISO 9000 quality standard. Measuring the number of
customer complaints is therefore often included in the
customer perspective of the Balanced Scorecard.

You want this measure to encourage your staff to treat each
complaint as an opportunity to learn from their mistakes
and implement corrective action which will prevent the
problem recurring.

However, you could find a situation where people fail to
log customer complaints in an attempt to hide them.
There is also the problem of deciding what a customer
complaint is. Customers who take the trouble of writing
to the quality manager usually get their complaint
recorded and dealt with, but what happens about the
irate telephone call taken by the customer service desk
and what happens to the informal criticism made during a
sales visit? It is therefore very important that everyone has a
clear view of the definition of a customer complaint and that
there is a quick and easy system of recording complaints.

Finally, management's attitude to customer complaints is
going to be very important. If there is strong pressure to
drive down the number of complaints or the general feeling
that customer complaints are a nuisance, then don't be
surprised if the number of complaints drops.

Internal process – first time yield (see figure 9)
First-time yield is a term used in manufacturing to describe
the amount of good quality product produced by a process
at the first attempt.

Performance Measurement Record Sheet

Measure	Customer complaints
Purpose	To understand which aspects of our performance upsets our customers so that we can continually improve our service
Relates to	The need for the business to satisfy its existing customers and to retain their custom in the future
Target	Maintain a customer complaint ratio of under 1% during 2000
Formula	$$\frac{\text{Number of customer complaints}}{\text{Number of customer orders despatched in the period}} \times 100$$
Frequency	To be measured and reviewed monthly
Who measures?	Sue Williams, Quality Manager
Source of data	The customer complaints system
Who acts on the data?	Sue Williams, Quality Manager
What do they do?	Analysis complaints by key process, ensures process owners conduct root cause analysis and complete corrective actions. Flag any major trends
Notes and comments	We need to ensure that all customer complaints are captured by the customer complaints system and that staff are regularly reminded about the customer complaints procedure

Figure 8, Customer complaints

It is important for several reasons:

- scrap is wasteful and expensive
- rework to rectify the mistake costs money
- rework takes capacity which could have been used to increase overall production
- inconsistencies in first-time yield can cause planning problems leading to uncertain delivery and customer dissatisfaction.

Improving first-time yield therefore has a wide range of benefits for your business. If you can collect the data correctly, measuring first-time yield is relatively straightforward. The main difficulties lie in:

- ensuring that all rework is measured
- ensuring that all the processes are included in the measure

Two examples come to mind to illustrate the first point. Firstly, one colleague exploring the rework figures in a shipyard discovered that any rectification taking less than two hours was excluded from the performance measure. As a result, despite the rework level being reported as only 5%, the general manager believed the company had to design and build a ship twice before it was delivered. Secondly, a former colleague told me how, as a young apprentice, he had fallen asleep on the night shift and let his lathe bore a hole right though a very large piston head which had taken weeks to make. To cover his tracks, he had machined the rest into swarf and as a result a six foot piston was 'lost on shop floor'.

Performance Measurement Record Sheet

Measure	Process first time yield
Purpose	To measure the rate of improvement in our production efficiency
Relates to	The need to reduce waste, minimise rework, control production and reduce costs
Target	Achieve a first time yield rate of 95% by the end of 2000
Formula	The produce of $\left(\dfrac{\text{Number of good quality products}}{\text{Number of units processed}} \times 100 \right)$ for all processes
Frequency	To be measured daily and reviewed monthly
Who measures?	Michael Johnson, Production Manager
Source of data	Daily process report sheets
Who acts on the data?	Stan Grey, Production Controller
What do they do?	Ensure route cause analysis is undertaken and corrective actions are planned, implemented and the impact reviewed
Notes and comments	Target to be reviewed at the end of the year. We also need to monitor the impact of the operator SPC training initiative

Figure 9, Process first-time yield

Turning to the second point, the formula is important.
Often first-time yield is calculated as the average of the
yields achieved. More accurately, it should be calculated as
the product of the yields (see example below).

Example of first-time yield calculations

Machine A	90%
Machine B	85%
Machine C	95%
Machine D	90%
Average yield	90%
Actual yield	65.41% $(.9 \times .85 \times .95 \times .9)$

Innovation and learning – new knowledge (see Figure 10)
Innovation and learning is always difficult to measure and
measuring the creation of new knowledge presents
particular difficulties. One way of measuring this used by a
number of larger companies is by the measurement of
patent approvals.

The desired outcome from this measure is that the new
patents reflect the generation of new knowledge in the
business and that staff are motivated to generate new
knowledge and so create new patents.

However, the number of patents could also be increased by:

- patenting discoveries which aren't important
- patenting discoveries too early, jeopardising the
  exploitation of the new discovery
- looking for discoveries which are patentable rather
  than useful to the future development of the
  business.

Patents also have the side effect of making public the discovery, so the adoption of 'patent approvals' as a key performance measure may also have the undesired side effect of informing your competitors exactly what line of research you are focusing on and how far you have advanced.

To avoid this, you may put a number of controls in place to ensure that discoveries are patented only when they meet certain criteria, or are passed by a review committee. The resulting performance measure may therefore look like Figure 10.

Designing groups of measures

Although it is useful to consider the design of each measure individually, you will find that measures often overlap in their application. It is not uncommon for more than one measure to be used to track one dimension of performance.

For example:

- employee satisfaction may be measured on an annual basis, but absenteeism or staff turnover may be used as proxy-measures of employee satisfaction between annual surveys
- customer satisfaction may be measured on an annual basis, but internal measures, such as on-time delivery, customer complaints and customer returns, may all be used as proxy-measures of customer satisfaction.

Performance Measurement Record Sheet

Measure	Number of new patent applications submitted
Purpose	To measure and encourage the creation of new knowledge
Relates to	The need for the business to innovate and create new products which are patent protected
Target	Achieve a rate of 6 patent applications per month by the end of 2000
Formula	Number of patent applications filed each month
Frequency	To be measured monthly, to be reviewed quarterly
Who measures?	Peter White, Technical Director
Source of data	Patent application log
Who acts on the data?	Peter White and his technical team
What do they do?	Manage the innovation process
Notes and comments	Remember to review patent application quality at year end, also, next year we may consider changing the measure to 'patents granted'

Figure 10, Patent applications submitted

In both these cases, the cost of measuring (doing the survey more often) or the problem of survey fatigue (people getting tired of answering questionnaires) means that you have to use other measures between surveys. However, you must remember that these are only proxies for the real measure, and the proxies should be re-calibrated as often as is practical to check that they actually reflect your real measure.

Summary

Deciding what to measure is not enough. You must also take care in designing the measures themselves. The key points to remember are:

- think about the behaviour you want to encourage
- define precisely what it is you are measuring
- make sure *all* data is collected, and collected in a consistent way
- achievement of the target stated in the measure must support at least one of the organisation's top line objectives
- take some time to find out how the results of the measures relate to each other°

Displaying and using the measures

So far we have looked at reasons for using the Balanced
Scorecard, what you should measure and how to measure.
This chapter concentrates on how to use the results to
improve the performance of your business.

The following pages will show ways of:

- displaying the measures and communicating what
  they mean
- making best use of the information
- ensuring positive action is taken to improve
  performance

Displaying the measures

The way in which the measures are displayed will have an
effect on how important they are perceived to be and how
seriously individuals regard subsequent actions to be taken.
They should be displayed professionally and in a public
place where everyone can see them without going out of
their way, such as the staff canteen, the reception area and
open plan offices. James Walker, a company based in
Cockermouth that manufactures seals and compression
packings, displays measures on boards in the company
colours. Ai Qualitek, a Cambridge-based manufacturer of
leak detection equipment, displays their nine key measures
on the wall in the staff canteen.

If there are measures that are specific to a particular
location then they need to be displayed as close as possible

to the people who can have a direct impact on the performance of that area.

The way in which information is displayed will affect how well it is used. Consider what particular method of display would be most appealing to the target group. If your measures are being displayed in the accounts department, for example, it might be helpful to show the supporting figures. In other departments these figures might just confuse the issue. For most people pictures are better than words or numbers and attractive colours help to make the information more memorable.

Credibility and integrity of information are vital if the results of measures are to be taken seriously and acted upon. Graphs that are out of date, figures that are changed because they are subsequently found to be incorrect or attempts to hide bad news all detract from the impact of the measures. In the light of this, you may decide at the outset not to display certain measures. Issues of confidentiality may arise if your display is in an area frequented by visitors, although there are ways of overcoming confidentiality issues by showing percentage of target rather than actual figures. In some cases, by displaying everything, you will create information overload and thus diminish the impact of the message. Whatever you decide, the important point is to be consistent.

Communicating the meaning of the measures
If positive action is to be taken after analysing the measures then everyone concerned with improving performance needs to understand fully what the results mean. At the beginning, briefing meetings should be held to explain what the Balanced Scorecard is and to gain commitment. The next stage in the communication process is to brief everyone concerned about the results of the measures and what these mean for the business. Exactly who is involved in these sessions will depend on the scope of the measures, but in principle, anyone from the Managing Director to the cleaner who sweeps the factory floor can affect performance.

Using the information

On Sunday we looked at some of the positive results that can be achieved by using the Balanced Scorecard, such as stimulating action in key areas, communicating direction and facilitating learning. Here are some simple, practical examples of ways in which the results of the measures can be used.

(a) Indicating trends
Many measurement systems look backwards to what has already happened. If it is constructed in the right way, some of the measures in your Balanced Scorecard should point to

the future and help you to predict trends so you can take remedial action at an earlier date. At the Chartered Management Institute, we measure the number of enquiries for our short course brochure each month. This is a good predictor of bookings to come, so if the enquiry rate has dropped we can take action by sending out additional mailshots for our courses. At Ai Qualitek the number and value of quotations is a predictor of value of business placed in the next three months. They can use this information to alert sales representatives to take any necessary action to improve business.

(b) Correlating results
The results of measures can be correlated to draw conclusions and determine action – although you must take care not to make spurious connections.

Speakers on Chartered Management Institute courses who attract the highest quality ratings from participants also attract the highest number of repeat bookings and therefore they have the best attended courses. This is the case (almost) irrespective of the subject of the course. The action we take from this is to use the highest quality speakers and to put in place a system for showing any downward trend in performance of individual speakers. By doing this we can catch potential problems before they cause serious damage.

A major airline has shown direct correlation between willingness of customers to recommend their service to others and sales revenue. Sears Roebuck have correlated customer satisfaction, employee satisfaction and revenue. Both organisations can use these results to concentrate effort on actions that will give them the best return.

(c) Year on year comparison

If you are persistent and consistent you can use the results of the Balanced Scorecard measures to build a good bank of data over time. This is invaluable in determining what is happening in your business. At the Chartered Management Institute, for example, we now have five years' data on number of enquiries and bookings placed. Whereas before, when these numbers dipped we would attribute the drop to 'The Christmas Holidays' or 'The Summer' or some other occasion, we can now look back to the corresponding time in years gone by and make a more informed judgement about the cause.

Reviewing and acting on the measures

It is important to get into the habit of regularly reviewing the performance measures. This should be done by the whole team in a group meeting. You will find this difficult at first as it takes time to set up the measures and often the first couple of meetings can be frustrating when the data simply isn't available. Your persistence will overcome this hurdle.

In reviewing individual measures ask the following questions:

- What is our current performance?
- How does actual performance compare with the target set?
- What are the main reasons why the target isn't being met?
- What is the plan for corrective action?
- Has the action been taken?
- Does the action have the desired impact on the results of the measures

You will find it useful to construct a picture or visualisation to help the review process. We have included two examples here, Ford QOS (a quality operating system originally developed by Ford Electronics) and a framework developed by Xerox.

Ford QOS
The visualisation developed by Ford comprises four panels on the same sheet (see Figure 12). These panels are:

- panel 1 – the graph of actual performance against target
- panel 2 – a breakdown of that result by the main factors contributing to the result achieving or missing the target
- panel 3 – the action planned to improve the performance
- panel 4 – the record of the impact of action taken

The idea of this visualisation is that performance is measured, the causes of under-performance are identified, action is planned, implementation of the action is verified and then the performance is measured again.

In this way, using Ford QOS closes the loop, ensuring performance measures are regularly reviewed and acted upon.

Xerox's follow-up framework
In the early 1990s, Xerox developed its management system to include a framework for its performance measures (see Figure 13). The framework includes:

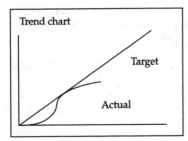

Figure 12, The Ford QOS measure visualisation (adapted from Neely et al, 1996)

- an owner, that is an individual responsible for preparing quarterly analysis of the trends, causes, strengths and areas for improvement as well as the action plan
- a sponsor: in Xerox's case, a main board director
- a desired state, including the results, approach and pervasiveness and a 7 point rating where 7 is 'world class' performance
- performance
- causal analysis
- strengths
- areas for improvement
- detailed action plan

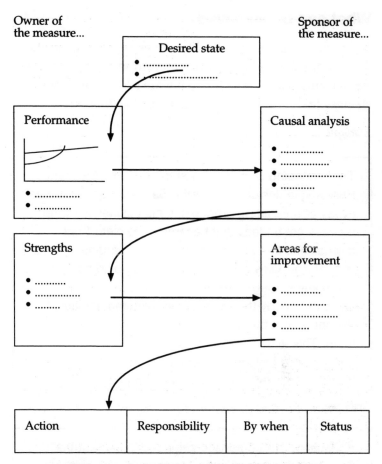

Figure 13, Follow-up of measures at Xerox (adapted from Olve et al, 1999)

The day-to-day use of the Xerox framework is very similar to closing the loop described for Ford. However, Xerox also takes a more strategic view by annually reviewing its measures as part of its self-assessment exercise, comparing and sharing performance across its own business units and making comparisons with other companies.

What can be achieved

It is clear that the measures themselves are useful, but the process of using the Balanced Scorecard in itself can have far-reaching results. The following are some examples of changes that have taken place in real companies.

Example 1

The Managing Director of a small systems company in East Anglia decided to use the Balanced Scorecard as a way of measuring progress in his business. As the process got underway it became quite clear from discussions that several of the senior managers had a very narrow view of the business and could not grasp some key strategic issues facing the business. In order to remedy the situation he recruited additional members with broader vision to strengthen the top team. This allowed some real increases in performance including an improvement in on-time delivery from 28% to 100% in eight months.

Example 2

A Midlands-based service company found that the Balanced Scorecard helped to change their culture from one that was bureaucratic and process-oriented to one where individuals used their own initiative and were results-oriented. Business results were regularly reported at staff meetings but had little meaning for the majority of people and were greeted with a big yawn. When those individuals became involved in working out the results of measures and therefore had a deeper understanding of their meaning; when they could see results presented graphically and realised that they could make an impact, they started to take a closer interest and make positive proposals for improving the business.

Example 3

The Managing Director of a medium sized manufacturing company found he was not getting commitment from his senior managers to implement the business strategy. He used the Balanced Scorecard as a means of putting a practical edge into the strategy discussions and, by doing this, improved both the strategy and the performance of the business. The senior team had more commitment to implementing the strategy because they felt they had played a part in its formulation. They now knew what was required of them and what the measures of success would be. The result was a significant increase in customer service and profitability

Some of the pitfalls

Having shown examples of companies in which the Balanced Scorecard has enabled really positive changes to take place, it is only fair to point out some of the pitfalls.

The main problems are:

(a) The amount of time taken

This is probably the most frequent problem and is worth considering at the early stages when you are drawing up the measures. Some measures are very easy to calculate because the data already exists in an easily accessible form. Others are more difficult because you have to set up new systems for collecting data or you have to collect data from several different areas. There are also the occasional measures such as surveys which can be very time consuming. When deciding what to measure, give some thought to the amount of time each measure will take – if it is very time consuming is it *really* worthwhile or can it be measured less often?

(b) People don't want the measures

Concern about what will happen if results aren't good can lead to distortion of the figures or excuses as to why the measures are no good. Of course some of these excuses might be genuine, particularly at the early stages before wrinkles have been ironed out. The important point is for individuals to see that the results are being used objectively for improving the business and not to allocate blame.

(c) Results are not what they seem
No matter how carefully you design your measures, problems in collecting the data can distort the results.

One company had two measures for delivery time. The first was on-time despatch. How many times were goods despatched on the due date? There was no dispute about this because the goods were either despatched on the appointed day or they weren't. The other measure, however, led to a great deal of debate. This was the measure of delivery lead time – how long it took between taking the order and despatch. It was found that orders placed through the branch sales network were not being put on to the sales order processing system immediately – unlike orders taken through head office – and this was creating an unfair discrepancy in the relative lead times. It was not until this was corrected that the measure became meaningful.

(d) Not involving enough people in the process
The success stories described earlier show the importance of involving a wide range of people in the process. If only a small number of people are involved there is narrower ownership and less commitment to taking action.

(e) Information overload
Try and limit the number of measures you review regularly. If you install too many measures, you will lose your focus.

Summary

In this chapter we have looked at how to make good use of the Balanced Scorecard process and at some of the problems you may encounter.

- How you display the measures will affect how seriously they are regarded and ultimately how successful the process is
- Regular monitoring is important to ensure information is up to date and is being acted upon
- Measures can be used in many different ways. At a macro level the process can help to create changes in culture. At the level of the measures themselves they provide early indicators of trends and comparisons with earlier levels of performance, and can reveal information on factors affecting your business which you might not otherwise have considered
- The main pitfalls are:
  - lack of time – this should be considered at the design stage
  - not involving enough people – putting the burden on too small a group and not creating wide enough commitment
  - not looking closely enough at the way in which data is gathered – which can lead to spurious results
  - information overload – keep to measures you can really use

Keeping your scorecard relevant

On Monday we talked about creating the right environment for launching a Balanced Scorecard initiative. On Tuesday we described how you should decide what to measure and on Wednesday we went on to discuss the design of the measures themselves. Yesterday we talked about reviewing the measures and the visualisations you can use to bring your measures alive. Today we are going to show how to keep your scorecard relevant and useful. This is particularly important because, in the longer term, as the environment changes and as the business develops, the scorecard has to change, adapt and grow as well, or it will die.

The two main themes for this chapter are:

- keeping the scorecard relevant
- weaving the process into the fabric of the business

Renewing and updating

Figure 14 shows the stages in the development of a Balanced Scorecard which we have discussed so far this week. It also shows the renewal routines which need to be put in place to keep the scorecard alive. These are:

(a) updating the target
(b) updating the measures
(c) changing the measures
(d) challenging the strategy

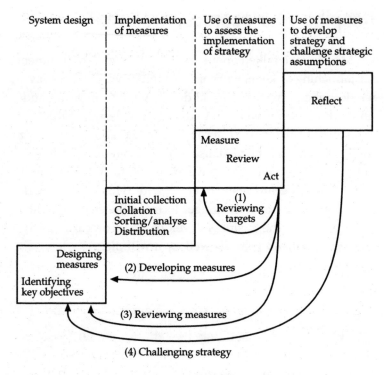

| System design | Implementation of measures | Use of measures to assess the implementation of strategy | Use of measures to develop strategy and challenge strategic assumptions |

Reflect

Measure

Review

Act

Initial collection
Collation
Sorting/analyse
Distribution

(1) Reviewing targets

Designing measures

(2) Developing measures

Identifying key objectives

(3) Reviewing measures

(4) Challenging strategy

Figure 14, Stages in developing and renewing the Balanced Scorecard

(a) Updating the targets

When a target is being reached and surpassed on a regular basis, the target needs to be reviewed. This happens automatically for many business performance measures as part of the annual budgeting process. Sales last year were £3 million, so next year the budget is increased to £3.5 million to account for inflation, the new customers who are now starting to buy our products, and so on.

However, this process should be carried out for all measures. If on-time delivery has now reached 90%, is it right to leave the target at that, or should it be increased to 95%? Rework last year fell to below 10%, so do we continue the trend by setting more challenging targets for the forthcoming year? Often in the budgeting process we concentrate on how much we can increase prices, increase the volume of sales and improve productivity. However, we fail to improve the targets for other performance measures, such as customer service, process improvements and innovation and learning, most of which are the performance drivers which allow us to improve our processes, win more customers and increase our productivity.

Therefore, as performance increases we need to review and update our targets.

(b) Updating the measure
Here we will look at an example of how measures may change over time and need updating.

The management team of a company has decided to introduce a suggestion scheme as a means of contributing towards its continuous improvement initiative.

They decide that the success of the scheme will be measured by the number of suggestions made each month. This will monitor the employees' commitment and involvement in the new initiative. However, once the scheme has been running for six months or so, with the number of suggestions increasing, the team realises that just encouraging suggestions is not sufficient. The suggestions need to be reviewed.

Consequently, a new measure is put in place, 'the number of suggestions reviewed in the month'. However, many suggestions are rejected during the review and so the management team realises that more emphasis should be put on the quality of the suggestions. They change the measure to read 'the number of suggestions accepted for implementation'.

By now they have a continuous flow of good suggestions, but still no action has taken place. The measure is modified once more to 'the number of suggestions implemented'.

What is being described here is a series of changes in the measure as the situation develops. Simply implementing a final measure isn't the answer in this case. You need to begin by encouraging people to make suggestions and the original measure does this. You then need to move the emphasis from the number of suggestions to the reviewer. Quality and not quantity will then become the issue. This will not happen until you have reached the stage of widespread involvement and have a system in place to evaluate the suggestions quickly. Finally, you get to the stage of measuring something really useful, the number of suggestions actually implemented and adding real value to the business. Starting with this measure may well have meant that the scheme never succeeded at all as there were too many barriers to success.

This example shows that, as the situation improves, measures should be reviewed and re-focused to ensure improved performance.

(c) Changing the measures
Apart from updating the measures because of internal improvements, measures must also be changed to reflect changes in strategy.

If your emphasis is moving from competing on cost to

competing on speed of response, the measures need to be changed to reflect this. In fact, each time you review and update your strategic plan, the measures should also be reviewed to ensure they remain congruent. This may well mean dropping some well-established measures and implementing new ones. If this isn't done, don't be surprised if the strategy fails, The old measures and reporting system will ensure that what has been decided is never implemented.

Let's take the example of the move from cost-based competition to speed of response. This looks at first glance to be a simple change but what you will find is a whole set of entrenched performance measures which work against it. When you are focusing on cost, machine utilisation is important and so is labour efficiency. The production department will have instigated systems which focus on developing longer runs of production in order to minimise the changeover costs from one product to another and to get all the benefits from stability. Speed of response, on the other hand, requires excess capacity and under-utilised resources so that you have the flexibility to respond when the customer requires it. It may also require smaller job lots and even batches of one-offs.

Implementing measures of responsiveness, such as 'reduction in average lead-time' may well measure at the top level how well you are implementing your strategy, but without taking out the lower-level measures of labour and machine efficiency the strategy will struggle. The answer is to change the lower-level measures to align with the new strategy. Introducing a measure which captures improvements in flexibility – such as the speed of

changeover or the skill matrix which monitors how many different jobs each individual can undertake – will help to refocus effort in the right direction.

As strategy changes, the measures need to change to reflect this strategy. But don't forget to realign the measures right down into the organisation and remove the measures which are in conflict with the new strategy, replacing them with more supportive measures.

(d) Challenging the strategy

Measures can be used to monitor the implementation of the strategy. In the example above, they trace the improvement in staff flexibility and speed of product changeover, through to the reduction in lead times. These are all steps in charting the implementation of the strategy. But one question remains, 'Is the strategy right?' In this case, is the reduction in lead time translating itself into increased sales, higher levels of customer satisfaction and, ultimately, profitable growth? The measures should tell you this and therefore challenge the strategy you are implementing.

In a different example, a chain of convenience stores was concerned about losing market share to the large supermarket chains. The management's strategy for counteracting this threat was to develop a customer care programme. They believed that if they could create an environment which was 'the friendly local corner shop' they could use the friendliness of the staff to promote the business and create a group of loyal customers.

The management therefore embarked on an intensive training programme throughout the country to train their staff in making eye contact with the customer, saying 'good morning' and other behaviour which would make the customer feel special. However, they didn't leave it there. They decided that they should measure the impact of the training programme and the change in the behaviour of their staff. This was done by mystery shoppers who went into a sample of the stores and measured the number of eye contacts, good mornings and so on.

When the data was analysed, the results shocked the management. Shops which had the lowest 'customer-friendly score' were the best performers in terms of sales per square foot and vice versa. Further study showed that there were times of the day when shops were particularly busy. At these times, the customers and staff colluded to give the customer what they wanted, quick service through the till. This was done by discouraging chatter through avoiding eye contact and greetings which encouraged conversation. Shops which didn't do this irritated their customers by keeping them waiting whilst so called 'customer-friendly activities' took place. The result was a reassessment of the strategy, a focus on providing maximum staffing at peak times of the day to minimise waiting and a re-focusing of the customer care programme to provide extra service outside the rush hours.

What this example shows is the way in which performance measures can and should be used to facilitate learning. It is important to reflect occasionally on what your performance measures are telling you about both the implementation of your strategy and the validity of the strategy itself. Challenging your strategy in this way is an important part of the performance measurement process.

Weaving the process into the fabric of your business

Another important way to keep your scorecard going is to weave it into the everyday processes of your business rather than to regard it as an initiative in itself.

A manufacturing company had put considerable effort into training in continuous improvement and the philosophy of Total Quality Management. However, they hadn't implemented any measures that linked TQM to business performance. They used the Balanced Scorecard to do this, introducing the idea that the Balanced Scorecard was the next step in implementing TQM. In this way the Balanced Scorecard process was seen as adding value to what they were already doing by demonstrating some positive benefits of TQM to business performance.

The danger is that if you create the Balanced Scorecard as a separate initiative it will receive attention only for a short time and will then fade when the next fad appears on the horizon. If you can link initiatives or processes together so that they are complementary you develop a certain strength and cohesion and the positive results are cumulative. This helps to build management competence in running the business.

Summary

Today we have looked at ways in which to keep your scorecard relevant. We have also talked about weaving the scorecard process into other initiatives (past and future) to ensure you build your management competence rather than lurching from one initiative to the next. The main points are:

- ensure you review and update your targets regularly
- update the measures as your performance improves
- change your measures in line with your strategy
- use the measures to monitor the success of your strategy

Beyond the Balanced Scorecard

During the week we have looked at the development of the Balanced Scorecard from creating the right environment, using it to improve performance, to keeping the scorecard alive in the longer term.

Today we will:

- review how a number of companies have adapted the scorecard to suit their own business needs
- look at some shortcomings of the Balanced Scorecard and propose an alternative
- finish with a summary of the week.

PURRFECTLY BALANCED CAT SHOW

Balanced performance measurement frameworks

Two questions are often asked about the Balanced Scorecard:

- are the perspectives of the Balanced Scorecard the right four perspectives?
- is the Balanced Scorecard complete?

What the Balanced Scorecard does is highlight four different perspectives of the business and makes us think about the difference between:

- financial and non-financial measures
- internal and external measures of success
- outcome measures and input measures

This is summarised in Figure 15 overleaf.

The Balanced Scorecard does have two main advantages. Firstly it is simple with only four perspectives. Secondly, it is now being widely used and accepted.

However, many companies have adapted the Balanced Scorecard to meet their own needs and some good examples are illustrated below.

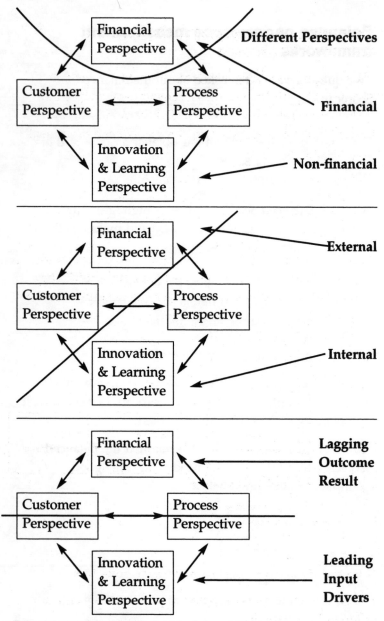

Figure 15, Different perspectives of the Balanced Scorecard

Examples of companies adapting the Balanced Scorecard

Many larger companies who have adopted a balanced approach to performance measurement have adapted the approach to their own situation, slightly modifying the concept in the process. We will show you some prominent examples here.

ABB
ABB are a large industrial conglomerate formed in 1988 through the merger of Asea of Sweden with BBC Brown Boveri of Switzerland.

ABB have developed five perspectives for their scorecard: process, employee, innovation, customer and profit. They display the perspectives in such a way as to emphasise the relationship between them (see Figure 16).

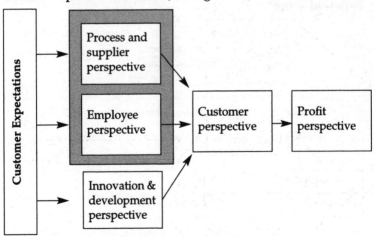

Figure 16, ABB's scorecard (adapted from Ewing & Lundahl, 1996)

The ABB framework is designed to put emphasis on the different time periods:

- innovation takes the longest to make an impact on the customer perspective
- improvements in the processes and employee perspectives impact the customer perspective in the next period
- improvements in the customer perspective impact the profit perspective in the next period

Skandia's Navigator

Skandia, a Swedish insurance company, developed a performance measurement framework known as the 'Skandia Navigator' (see Figure 17). This framework combines its scorecard with its view of intellectual capital. In the Navigator a fifth perspective, 'Employee Focus', has been added to the conventional four perspectives of the Balanced Scorecard.

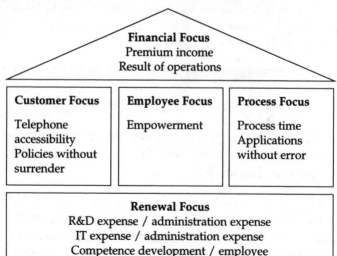

Financial Focus
Premium income
Result of operations

Customer Focus	**Employee Focus**	**Process Focus**
Telephone accessibility Policies without surrender	Empowerment	Process time Applications without error

Renewal Focus
R&D expense / administration expense
IT expense / administration expense
Competence development / employee

Figure 17, Skandia AFS's Business Navigator (adapted from Skandia's web site)

Skandia sees employees as the link between the other perspectives. For example, process performance doesn't solely depend on the systems and procedures used in the organisation, it also depends on the skills, knowledge and competence of the people applying the process. Similarly, the customer and the renewal focuses can only be delivered through people. As a result, 'Employee Focus' is the Navigator's central box.

DHL

DHL are providers of international air-express parcel services. Their vision of the future was developed over a 12 month period by the Board of Directors who spent one day a month in workshops. They started by considering the business under the four perspectives of the Balanced Scorecard: financial, external customer, internal process and innovation and learning. However, the Board wanted the language they used to be accessible to the whole business. To achieve this, they articulated their performance management framework as follows:

> 'We have customers, to whom our people provide a service, through following processes, which, when successful, produce results.'

Subsequently, they split the customer perspective into the two elements the customer sees: the core service and the ease of use of that service.

The result was a vision of what the company will look like in the future for each of the four perspectives. This was brought together with a specific set of high-level actions and underpinning projects to take the company forward. These were supported by measures and targets which

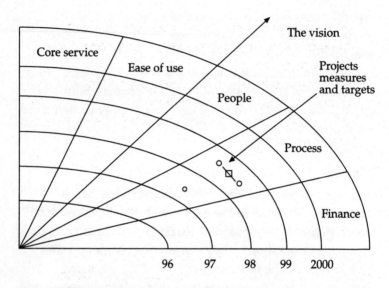

Figure 18, The DHL vision (adapted from Bourne, 1999)

monitored progress towards the vision as well as measures to run the business day to day.

James Walker

James Walker are manufacturers and world wide suppliers of gaskets and compression packings to industries as diverse as medical appliances and nuclear power. James Walker developed a Balanced Scorecard for their plant in Cockermouth which comprised four business units and six major service functions.

In order to develop a balanced set of measures for each service function, a process was developed which took the management team of each of the functions through a series of exercises. These exercises helped them identify:

- who their internal customers were and to quantify the goals and targets they needed to achieve to satisfy these customers
- the suppliers on whom they were dependent and measures of supplier performance
- their internal processes and measures of efficiency and effectiveness.

This created the customer, internal supplier and process perspectives. The financial perspective was taken from the budget and the innovation and learning perspective from their ongoing development programme.

At the end of this process, each service function had a balanced set of measures developed and agreed by the senior management team. These were in the form of a five box scorecard as shown in Figure 19 overleaf.

Adapting the scorecard
We have illustrated how the Balanced Scorecard is taken and adapted during its implementation in organisations. Many of the companies shown above are large, but the James Walker example was included to show that even small to medium-sized organisations can adapt the scorecard successfully.

If your organisation does want to modify the scorecard this is usually a good sign. It demonstrates that the people involved are taking ownership and this has to be a good omen for future success.

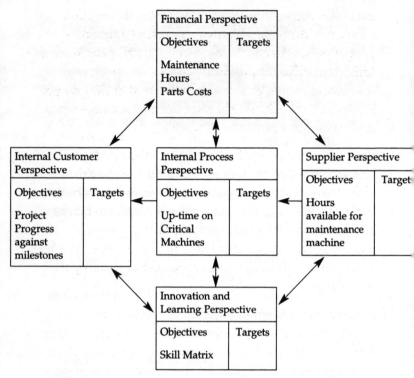

Figure 19, James Walker's Balanced Service Scorecard (adapted from Bourne & Wilcox, 1998)

Shortcomings of the Balanced Scorecard

Although the scorecard is popular, it is by no means without shortcomings. Companies adapting the scorecard to their own needs have addressed some of these, but there are still five key shortcomings that you need to be aware of.

1 People are excluded. The innovation and learning perspective is often translated into a 'people' perspective, or a people perspective is added as in the

examples above, but it is excluded from the original scorecard. We would highly recommend adopting a people perspective for two reasons. Firstly, people are an important driver of performance and, secondly, not measuring people gives the impression that they do not matter to the business–not something to promote when implementing a new way of working.

2   Suppliers are excluded. Many companies are dependant on their suppliers. In manufacturing it is often the largest cost element. In financial services IT provision is being increasingly outsourced, but it is still critical to business success. Scorecard proponents argue that suppliers should be considered within the Process Perspective, but this approach does not give suppliers the visibility they now deserve.

3   Regulators are ignored. Increasingly, companies are being subjected to regulation. The FDA has an immense impact on the fortunes of drug companies, the FAA on aviation and the Health and Safety Executive on nearly every business. These are non-negotiable standards which have to be met, but do not fit into the Balanced Scorecard's framework.

4   Community and environmental issues are missing. Many companies may believe that these are not important to them, but several high profile cases should make companies at least consider this perspective. Shell, despite their scientific risk assessment, ran into serious problems with disposing of their platform 'The Brent Spar' in the North Sea. Similarly, many UK retail banks have come under intense pressure in recent years as a

direct result of their branch rationalisation programmes. Nowadays environmental issues and local communities are closely linked and companies need to measure and monitor the impact they are having. If they do not, they many find themselves subject to attack by pressure groups who can damage the companies' reputation, interrupt trading and ultimately destroy the business.

5 Competitors are ignored. The Balanced Scorecard views the external environment through the eyes of the shareholders and customers. Besides the stakeholders identified above, companies need to monitor the environment to track competitor activity and technology. The scorecard is designed to answer the question, 'Is the chosen strategy being implemented?' but fails to ask the question, 'Is the chosen strategy the right strategy for our business?' It does not highlight or track threats from non-traditional competitors.

These criticisms mainly stem from the fact that the Balanced Scorecard is not a multiple stakeholder framework. In most Western Societies today, other stakeholders cannot be ignored, as inevitably their action will impact on financial performance and shareholder value. Therefore any performance measurement framework needs to reflect the needs of all the important stakeholders.

The Performance Prism

The Performance Prism is an alternative framework jointly developed by the Centre for Business Performance at Cranfield School of Management and Accenture. It is a three dimensional model (see Figure 20).

The two stakeholder facets of the performance prism:

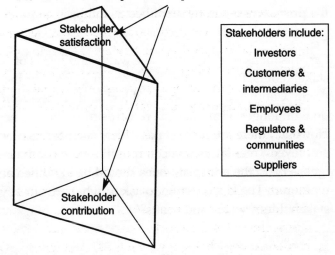

Stakeholders include:

Investors

Customers &
intermediaries

Employees

Regulators &
communities

Suppliers

The three internal facets of the performance prism:

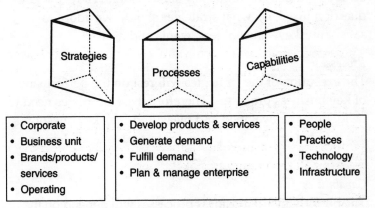

- Corporate
- Business unit
- Brands/products/
  services
- Operating

- Develop products & services
- Generate demand
- Fulfill demand
- Plan & manage enterprise

- People
- Practices
- Technology
- Infrastructure

Figure 20, The five facets of the performance prism

The Performance Prism has two ends, the *stakeholder wants and needs* and the *stakeholder contribution* as well as three faces, *strategies, processes and capabilities*. The way in which the prism works can be described as follows:

SWANS, stakeholder wants and needs?
Organisations exist to satisfy the wants and needs of stakeholders; therefore this is the starting point for the prism. Companies have shareholders so their needs are to do with longer term financial rewards from the business. However, there are other stakeholders such as customers, employees, regulators and communities who cannot be ignored and the important ones should be identified and measured. The key question to ask is 'what are our key stakeholders' wants and needs?'

Strategies
The strategies an organisation adopts should be related to achieving the needs of the key stakeholders. Here, the key question to ask is, 'what strategies should we adopt to satisfy our key stakeholders' wants and needs?'

Processes
The execution of the strategies will rest on the performance of key business processes. Therefore these processes need to be identified, developed and measured. The key question to ask is 'what are the key processes to enable us to deliver our strategies?'

Capabilities
The performance of business processes will depend on the capabilities which underpin them – skills of the people, technology employed, system, practices and infrastructure. To be successful, all these need to be identified, developed and measured. The key question to ask is 'what are the key capabilities that underpin the performance of our processes?'

OWANS, our wants and needs

The final piece is the bottom end of the prism; our wants and needs of our stakeholders. Stakeholder contribution is an essential ingredient of any successful business and so should be identified and measured. Take the example of employees; what they usually want from the company is pay, a safe environment, job security and some purpose in their work. However, what the organisation wants from them is their skills, energy and commitment. Too often these different facets get confused so it is useful to separate them and make the needs and contributions explicit. The key question to ask here is 'what contributions do we need from our stakeholders to make the organisations successful?'

Therefore, although the Performance Prism is a more complex framework than the Balanced Scorecard it does consider a much wider set of requirements and addresses many of the current criticisms of the scorecard.

A summary of the week

Here are 10 key points we hope you will take away from this book:

1. Financial measures of performance are not adequate on their own for managing your organisation – you need a balanced set of measures
2. The Balanced Scorecard has four perspectives: financial, customer, internal process and innovation and learning. For most organisations these represent an adequate set of perspectives for your performance measures

3. Another way to check your balance of measures is to consider

- financial measures v non-financial measures
- measures of internal performance v measures of external performance
- measures of drivers of performance v measures of outcomes
- historical measures of achievement v measures which help predict the future

4. The process you use to develop your performance measures is as important as the measures themselves. The process will develop an understanding of the strategy and a commitment to implement and use the Balanced Scorecard.

5. The process of developing a Balanced Scorecard will involve the senior management team investing time in debating the objectives and agreeing the measures. This can't be delegated so if they are unwilling to do it, don't start.

6. Measure what matters, develop your measures from your strategy and focus on the key success factors

7. Take the time to design measures which will support your strategy and create the right behaviour

8. Close the loop, manage your measures so that they are reviewed, analysed and acted upon.

9. Display your measures round your organisation so that everyone can see exactly what is happening. Making them visible takes them beyond the status

of 'management toy' to 'business wide
improvement tool'.
10. Be persistent, a successful Balanced Scorecard
    implementation may not bring you instant success
    but over time the benefits can be enormous

And finally, a statement made by one senior manager
reflecting on his experience:

> 'This is the single biggest improvement tool we have
> used. We moved further faster with this than with
> anything else.'

Good luck!

IF WE COULD JUST
CAPTURE THIS

For information

on other

IN A WEEK titles

go to

www.inaweek.co.uk